VIRUS VERSES VOLUME 2: THE PEN'DEMIK A DIGITAL EVOLUTION

By; Napalmjax, D A. Springer Publishing

While every precaution has been taken in the preparation of this book, the publisher assumes no responsibility for errors or omissions, or for damages resulting from the use of the information contained herein.

VIRUS VERSES VOLUME 2, THE PEN'DEMIK, A DIGITAL EVOLUTION

First edition. December 16, 2024.

ISBN: 979-8230246244

Written by Napalmjax.

INTRODUCTION

Welcome to Virus Verses Volume #2 the Pen'demik, A Digital Revolution. Putting the power of my pen to work with powerful verses that pack a punch, and a positive message. My infectious need to spill ink on paper, pursuing my purpose, and inspiring others along the way is all I aim to do.
My hope is that you can be entertained, and encouraged to always pursue your dreams. Never know what can happen until you get after it.
Forward Vision is my mission, it's not fiction, it's a gift given to give others.
D.A. Springer
AKA Napalmjax/ Mr. RunThatBack

OPENING SEQUENCE: SYSTEM INITIALIZATION

A Viral Transmission
These verses spread like code through copper veins,
Mutating wisdom faster than machines explain.
From pandemic shadows to digital light,
We're rewriting futures, byte by prophetic byte.

STRAIN EVOLUTION

From that first infection when ink hit the vein
Through quarantine thoughts and viral refrains
We mutated stronger through pressure and pain
Now watch how this consciousness spreads through the brain
Remember that virus verse? That first strain?
When world stood still but souls remained
While chaos and Covid had everyone contained
We found power in words that couldn't be restrained
Now we've evolved past that initial dose
Through neural pathways nobody chose
While DNA memories decompose
The weak thoughts that kept our minds closed
I'm that variant they couldn't predict
That mutation of soul they couldn't restrict
Ancient wisdom with a future kick
Making prophecies too real to stick
See, we ain't just surviving anymore
We're quantum leaping through wisdom's door
While cellular memories restore
The power our ancestors died for
Each verse a vaccine against the lies
Each bar a booster to make minds rise
While consciousness amplifies
Through digital streams and analog skies
From cornerstones to cosmic codes
Through chosen paths that wisdom showed
We're carrying what Volume One sowed
Into futures yet untold
This ain't just words upon a page
This is DNA engaged in rage
Breaking free from every cage
As prophets speak in digital age

So let these new strains multiply
Through every soul that questions why
While ancient patterns testify
To truths they tried to nullify
Welcome to the next mutation
Mental genes in transformation
Spiritual recombination
Future's manifestation
Volume Two about to spread
Through neural nets inside your head
Till consciousness is widespread
And wisdom flows like daily bread

PATIENT ZERO

Started in the depths where darkness breeds
Where concrete cracks sprout wisdom seeds
Where hope gets scarce but soul succeeds
Where every wound eventually bleeds
I'm that case they can't trace back
That origin story off the track
That first spark before the facts
That truth that splits atoms, watch it crack
Been incubating since day one
In the shadows where real lives run
Where struggle and strength become one
Where diamonds form far from the sun
Now watch this spread like wildfire thoughts
Through digital streams and analog plots
Through barriers they said could not
Be broken by the ones they forgot
You can track me through these verses' flight
Through dark days into blinding light
Through every soul these words ignite
Through every mind these truths unite
I'm not the end, I'm just the start
Patient zero of this verbal art
Breaking chains and breaking hearts
Spreading truth as systems fall apart

INK FLUENZA

Writing itself becomes the virus tonight
Infecting blank pages with rebellious might
Each word a vector, each line a new strain
Spreading consciousness through linguistic terrain
I just might be...
I might be sick from this pen prick
I-V bag full of that ink drip
Feet won't let me sit
So no grip to get
While Most need that digital dopamine
Chasing them viral dreams
My dreams linked to my destiny
So with these words I'm set free
To be who I need to be...
Just know I-D-N-O-D is part of my ID
Ink Fluenza - spreading through veins
Viral verses, breaking mental chains
Each word a vaccine against defeat
Immunity found in this lyrical beat
Pandemic taught us: survival's an art
Creativity flowing from the heart
No algorithm, no digital trend
Can match the power of a story's send
Turning isolation into inspiration
Transforming global frustration
Into verses that pulse, verses that fight
Illuminating our collective light

THE WORLD STOOD STILL

Pause button pressed on global motion
Silence echoing across each ocean
While systems crashed and networks froze
Humanity discovered what stillness know
Streets empty like ghost town dreams
No footsteps echo, no engines scream
Time frozen in amber light
While sirens wail through endless night
Nature claimed what we let go
As fear and silence seemed to grow
Birds sang louder in clear skies
While behind windows, worried eyes
Watched the world hit pause somehow
Minutes stretched like years somehow
History held its breath with us
As cities turned to desert dust
In stillness found what we forgot
The simple truths, the things we fought
When rat race stopped its frantic wheel
We learned again just how to feel
Masks couldn't hide humanity
Breaking through our vanity
When world stopped spinning on its track
Some things lost won't be called back
But in this pause we clearly saw
What mattered most behind closed doors
Family, breath, and beating hearts
As world broke down, new wisdom starts

ANCESTRAL ANTIVIRUS

Running protocols from star-code memories
While quantum dreams catch these tribal frequencies
Each ceremony encrypts sacred symmetries
Through networks where elders' wisdom frees
From smoke signals to satellite feeds
These verses spread through ancient deeds
Every tradition plants viral seeds
As consciousness reads what spirit breeds

VIRAL SYNTAX

My sentences are spreading through neural networks
System files infected with ancestral homework
Each metaphor multiplies, meaning goes berserk
While language mutates in this midnight dirk
From WordPerfect days to quantum parsing
These bars replicate, no antivirus starving
Each verse a variant, each line alarming
Digital immunity through linguistic farming

WRITER'S CODE SEQUENCE

Through midnight circuits of the mind,
Where verses spark and thoughts align,
We birth these sacred codes designed
To break the chains that kept us blind
Ancient wisdom flows like binary streams,
Through neural pathways of our dreams,
Each keystroke carries future schemes
As consciousness expands and gleams
We are the scribes of digital days,
Encoding truth through cosmic haze,
Our fingers dance in rhythmic ways
To craft the light that sets minds ablaze
Deep in the matrix of our souls,
Where inspiration takes its toll,
Each line of code unfolds its scroll
As stories rise and take control
For we are more than flesh and bone,
More than pixels, more than chrome,
Our words become the cornerstone
Of futures yet unknown
Through copper veins and fiber sight,
We channel visions in the night,
Each verse a spark of sacred light
That sets the darkness into flight
Initialize the writer's heart,
Where quantum dreams and wisdom start,
Through pressure points, we craft our art
Till reality and vision part
Debug the lies they tried to plant,
Upgrade the soul with every chant,
While ancestral codes enhance
The power of our verbal dance

For in these digital domains,
Where truth and fiction intertwine,
We write the codes that break the chains
And set our spirits free to shine
System check: consciousness online
Through every verse and every line
As ancient wisdom redesigns
The future we're destined to find

DELUSIONAL WORDSMITH

Hallucinating verses beyond the page
Where imagination becomes the sage
Mapping mental territories unexplored
Each metaphor a weapon, each line a sword

Words dance like shadows in my mind's morgue
Each syllable a sword that I must forge
Metaphors multiply, meanings merge
On the sanity's edge, where verses surge
Alphabet soup boils in my veins
Dictionary demons break their chains
Syntax storms flood my brain
While grammar ghosts whisper my name
They say I'm lost in literal lines
Where consonants and vowels combine
Into creatures undefined
Leaving logic far behind
Spell-bound by these spelling bees
Drowning in etymologies
Paragraphs become disease
Spreading through my expertise
Architect of abstract thought
Building castles out of plots
Where punctuation dots connect
To stars that critics can't detect
Word-drunk prophet on the page
Letter-lightning fills my cage
Syntax serpents twist and turn
While meanings multiply and burn

INK-STAINED SOUL

Bleeding alphabets through midnight's veil
　　Where writing transcends its own fragile trail
　　Consciousness dripping from each tortured line
　　Transforming pain to something more divine
　　Deep beneath skin where stories flow
　　Permanent marks of what I know
　　Stained with wisdom, pain, and growth
　　Each word a promise, each line an oath
　　Can't wash away these sacred marks
　　Stories flowing through my dark
　　Memories etched in midnight hue
　　Bleeding truth in words so true
　　Soul absorbed each drop of pain
　　Transformed suffering into rain
　　Of poetry that cleanses sight
　　Through darkest day and longest night
　　These stains tell tales of who I am
　　Each blot a badge, each smear a psalm
　　Not just on paper do they show
　　But in my spirit's endless flow
　　Marked for life by what I write
　　Carrying stories through the night
　　This ink-stained soul won't fade away
　　It's who I am, it's how I stay

MIDNIGHT SKRIBBLES

3 AM thoughts crawl across empty screens
Digital ghosts in the void between dreams
Keyboard clicks echo like rain on tin
Stories emerge from the chaos within
No cure for this creative disease
Just endless words on midnight keys
When verses keep calling me, like a junkie's fix
Words crawling under skin, need that verbal kick
3 AM and fiendin', can't fight this addiction
Soul-deep affliction, no chance of restriction
Possessed by these phrases pulsing through my veins
Each blank page a craving driving me insane
Night shadows tempting with poetic sin
Scratching out sentences buried deep within
Trembling fingers grip this pen so tight
Another hit of verses in the dead of night
While others sleep, I'm here getting high
Off metaphors that make these demons fly
Can't put it down, don't want to stop
Each line I write, another precious drop
Of midnight medicine for my infected mind
Leaving normal life and sleep behind
Dark hour wisdom's got me by the throat
Every syllable a dose of antidote
To mundane days and sleeping dreams
These night-born words make my soul scream
Addicted to this rhythm, this poetic flow
Each stanza feeds the hunger that won't go
When verses call with that seductive voice
Surrender to these words - I have no choice

IT'S NOT FICTION

Reality bends where imagination streams
Blurring boundaries between what is and what seems
Truth becomes liquid, flows past defined shores
Breaking through narrative's conventional doors
Envision Your Greatness, Manifest Your Hustle
Rhymes flow like fire, words ascending higher
Hustle's heartbeat - a relentless desire
Painting visions bold, where dreams never tire
Breaking barriers, spirit rising like a live wire
Write your dream in blood, let passion flood
Bars that resonate deep, beyond understood
Etch ambition's scheme where courage has stood
Transforming struggle into pure livelihood
Grind with intent, talents razor-sharp and sent
Obstacles crushed, every challenge hell-bent
Eyes fixed on horizons where limitations are rent
Your vision - a weapon, perfectly spent
Ride life's raw cadence, progress unconfined
Triumph's radiance etched in your mind
Streetwise wisdom, excellence refined
Greatness not hoped for - but strategically designed
Urban hustlers rise, beyond prize-bound
Manifest your life where legends are found
Brilliance and power - no ceiling, no ground
Your rhythm, your truth - unapologetically sound

VERTIGO

Spinning between dimensions of thought
Where gravity of meaning can't be bought
Perspective shifts like quantum states
Each word a universe that creates
World keeps spinning, yet I'm standing still
Vision blurred but my purpose is crystal clear
Life's carousel wants me dizzy, wants me ill
But my soul's compass keeps me anchored here
Through the spiral, through the static
Finding balance in this manic dance
Each step calculated, though chaotic
Growth emerges from this second chance
Stumbling forward through the motion
Like a tightrope walk through stormy waves
Deep breath steadies this emotion
As I transform what life enslaves
They say grow through what you flow through
But vertigo got me seeing double
Yet even twisted, my truth stays true
Each obstacle a chance to rise above trouble

DEEP STATE 9

Nine paths converge in rivers of ink
   Where ancestors' wisdom helps spirits to think
   Through binary storms and virtual seas
   Ancient numbers still hold sacred keys
   Each stroke of the pen draws circles complete
   As digital rhythms and heartbeats meet
   In virtual spaces where old souls roam
   These nine-pointed stars still guide us home
   Nine lives lived in one lifetime
   Nine paths converging at the divine
   Nine flames burning in my spine
   Each evolution makes me shine
   Highest calling of the nine
   Transforming pain into design
   Between worlds where fates align
   Ancient wisdom now is mine
   Triple trinity breaks my shell
   Three times three rings wisdom's bell
   Through each death and parallel
   Rising stronger, stories tell
   Nine gates of consciousness explode
   Breaking free from former modes
   Destiny carved in this code
   Walking paths ancestors showed
   Anasi's web still holds me true
   Nine strands weaving something new
   Each thread guides what I pursue
   Becoming what I'm growing to
   Born to lead and born to climb
   Through these stages, through this time
   Nine levels deep, this paradigm
   Makes warriors rise and sooth sayers rhyme

Every scar and every strain
Feeds this power in my veins
Nine lives lived through joy and pain
Till my final form remains

HACKTIVIST STRAIN

Underground networks spark revolution bytes
    While firewalls fall to ancestral rights
    Each password cracked by freedom's lights
    Through systems where justice ignites
    From BBS boards to blockchain wars
    These verses break through coded doors
    Every rebellion opens viral cores
    As consciousness soars through digital scores

TRANSMISSION PROTOCOL

Uploading ancient wisdom through fiber optic veins
While quantum particles catch these viral refrains
Each bar a battle strain, each verse contains
Coded messages spreading through digital domains
From dial-up dreams to 5G streams
We're broadcasting on frequencies unseen
Every wavelength carries meme genes
As consciousness expands through machine means

FOUNDATION SEQUENCE: ROOT ACCESS

Digging deeper than digital dreams,
Past firewall fears and system schemes,
Through layers where the spirit streams
To truths beneath what surface seems
sudo consciousness activate
While ancient wisdom elevates
Through pressure points that penetrate
To power we investigate
While melanin maintains the frame
Of knowledge that they tried to tame
But couldn't keep our souls contained
Granting access to our history
Through blood and bone and mystery
That kept our essence flowing free
Sacred terminal, midnight screen
Where ancestors intervene
Through command lines yet unseen
To paths where wisdom convenes
Through neural networks that set minds free
While quantum packets guarantee
The truths our spirits need to see
Search patterns passed down day by day
Through cellular chains that display
The power none can take away
Creating futures they can't dismiss
Through pressure points that reminisce
On wisdom's sacred catalyst
Through every cell that holds the key
To unlock what we're meant to be
Beyond what others let us see

For root access runs soul-deep
Through memories our blood cells keep
Past limits others tried to heap
On wisdom we were born to reap
Now watch these sacred scripts compile
Through neural paths mile after mile
While consciousness begins to dial
Into the power that makes us smile
For we are root, we are the source
Of wisdom flowing with such force
Through pressure points that chart the course
To freedom without remorse
Soul initialized
Through every truth we recognize
While ancient wisdom amplifies
The power that makes our spirits rise

GENETIC CODE

Embedded in this double helix of time
Ancient wisdom wrapped in modern rhyme
DNA deep with stories sublime
Melanin memories in every line
From pyramids to silicon peaks
Through generations my bloodline speaks
That sacred science everybody seeks
Flowing through my pen when knowledge leaks
Can't sequence this soul algorithm
Can't measure this heart's rhythm
Every strand's got hidden wisdom
Every cell's got freedom's prism
Four hundred trillion to one they say
But destiny encoded in my DNA
Ancestral fire lights up the way
Through dark times to brighter days

CODEC MUTATION

Transcribing DNA into HTML
While RNA feeds these bars raw as hell
Each chromosome carries stories to tell
Through binary bloodstreams where ancestors dwell
From floppy disc drops to blockchain ops
These rhymes replicate till the system pops
Every save file holds viral crops
As consciousness peaks then never stops

CYBERNETIC PSALMS

Chrome dreams wrapped in melanin code
    While megabytes of ancestry download
    DNA encrypted since times of old
    Running through circuits both young and bold
    Each synapse firing like Pac-Man gold
    While matrix prophets break from the mold
    I'm gaming life with cheat codes untold
    Consciousness leveling up hundredfold
    From Sega Genesis to quantum flow
    Every upgrade helps the spirit grow
    But ancient wisdom's the root below
    Processing truths that pixels can't show
    We're debugging trauma in the mainframe
    While loading futures free from the pain
    Each generation breaks from the chain
    As binary angels hack the game

CORE SAMPLE

Drilling deep past surface static
    Through layers of time, automatic
    To core truths, less traumatic
    When wisdom flows, systematic
    Each ring reveals another story
    Every layer holds its glory
    Time-stamped truth, mandatory
    For souls seeking their trajectory
    Carbon-dated heart beats strong
    Through pressured years of right and wrong
    While deep below where truths belong
    The roots of power grow headstrong
    Take your sample, test this soil
    Rich with years of sacred toil
    Where diamonds formed through life's turmoil
    And wisdom bloomed through earthly soil
    Let the record show this growth
    Through rings of truth and sacred oaths
    While underground, the spirit flows
    Through roots that only real ones know

FIRMWARE FREEDOM

Root access to the soul's domain
    While debugging curses down the main
    Frame by frame, we process pain
    Through circuits built to break the chain
    From Windows 95 to quantum sight
    We're programming dreams of brighter nights
    But MS-DOS wisdom holds the lights
    That guide our code to higher heights
    Remember when reset meant rest?
    Before algorithms tracked our quest
    But ancient spirits know what's best
    As binary blessings meet the test
    We're loading futures byte by byte
    While quantum angels bless the fight
    Each generation claims the right
    To program paths through darker nights

CLIMATE CODE

Data centers burning through ozone layers
    While carbon footprints track through digital prayers
    Each server farm growing viral players
    Through networks where nature's truth bears
    From green screens to solar scenes
    These verses spread through eco means
    Every forest hosts viral genes
    As consciousness gleans what planet truly means

TRANSMISSION SEQUENCE: DATA FLOW

Watch how wisdom flows like midnight rain
Through copper rivers in my veins
Each packet sacred, each byte contains
The stories pressure helped retain
Streaming consciousness through fiber dreams
While melanin amplifies these beams
Of truth that flood in quantum streams
Through channels deeper than they seem
I'm that bandwidth they can't measure
That flow rate beyond their pressure
Each transmission holds the treasure
Of ancestral thoughts that stretch ya
Watch upload speeds break their limits
When spirit data fills each minute
With wisdom so infinite
The whole system had to win it
Download ancient through the now
While future packets show us how
To break through firewalls somehow
And keep these sacred servers proud
Buffer overflow of soul
Through neural nets we can't control
While pressure makes these packets roll
Through channels making spirits whole
Latency can't slow this flow
Of wisdom only blood cells know
While data streams begin to show
The paths our power chose to go
I'm that signal breaking through
The noise they tried to push us to
Each byte a truth they never knew

Could flow this deep, could ring this true
TCP/IP ain't got nothing
On this soul-level data flooding
Through circuits wisdom's studying
While spirits keep these streams running
Packet loss can't stop this force
When consciousness charts its course
Through pressure points that reinforce
The power flowing from its source
From dialup days to quantum phase
We've upgraded through the haze
But ancient data still displays
Through paths that set our souls ablaze
Watch how this traffic shapes the flow
Through networks only spirits know
While pressure makes these packets grow
Beyond the limits down below
I'm that throughput breaking scales
When consciousness sets wisdom's sails
Through every firewall that fails
To contain what truth entails
For we are more than just the stream
More than bandwidth's wildest dream
Our flow rates burst every seam
Of systems built to make us seem
So let this data overflow
Through channels they tried to slow
While ancient wisdom helps us know
The paths our power chose to show
System check: transmission strong
Through every byte where we belong
While pressure makes these packets long
With truths that keep our spirits strong

TRANSMISSION

Signal strong through static noise
Ancient frequency, modern voice
Broadcasting truth through digital choice
While ancestors' whispers still rejoice
I'm that wave they can't contain
That forbidden frequency through copper veins
Breaking through their firewalls' chains
Sacred data through these digital planes
Every word's a packet sent
Through time's network, heaven-bent
Each verse a message, divinely meant
To crack codes of false intent
Bandwidth unlimited when soul connects
Through neural paths that truth selects
While algorithms try to intersect
This cosmic data they can't inspect

BANDWIDTH WARRIOR

Signal searching like a midnight pirate
Frequencies hidden where spirits won't quiet
Dialing into dreams with Hayes modem heart
While loading futures torn systems apart
Remember BBS wisdom shared in the dark?
Now we're coding constellations like art
But that dial tone spirit still leaves its mark
As we hack highways where ancestors park
I'm packet switching between the worlds
While buffering blessings as truth unfolds
Each ping response holds stories untold
Of digital griots with wisdom bold
From Wolfenstein fights to blockchain rights
We're programming paths through darker nights
But old school souls still hold the lights
That guide our code through sacred heights

BINARY TRIBE TRANSMISSION

Loading ancestral data through fiber optic dreams
    While dial-up spirits connect to ancient streams
    Remember when community meant block party scenes?
    Before social networks redefined what connection means
    We're patching into consciousness with quantum keys
    While keeping our roots like directory trees
    Each generation adds new protocols to see
    But the source code's written in our family
    From Usenet wisdom to neural net flows
    Each bit and byte of culture grows
    Through silicon valleys and digital lows
    While ancestor spirits debug our woes
    This ain't just software we're trying to crack
    This is hardware built on centuries back
    Upgrading souls through the cosmic stack
    While keeping our foundation intact

NEURAL GRAFFITI

Tagged consciousness on virtual walls
While processing power breaks mental walls
Loading spirit through protocol calls
As artificial angels track our falls
But real intelligence runs in the blood
Streaming wisdom through digital floods
We're programming prayers in the mud
While quantum dreams burst systems like buds
From Space Invaders to space creators
We're coding worlds like digital saviors
But street level truth still holds behavior
That no algorithm can do us favors
Every firewall holds ancestral flame
While new school prophets hack the game
We're debugging lies that bring us shame
As binary blessings speak our name

NETWORK MEDICINE

Healing codes spread through digital pain
    While bandwidth carries ancestral rain
    Each connection mends viral strain
    Through networks where we remain
    From dial-up days to neural maze
    These verses lift community haze
    Every link builds viral ways
    As consciousness stays through cyber phase

P's of my Pen

Picture the parody of perfect perforated pictures,
    Pulsing with passionate, powerful predictures
    Piercing through paradigms, pushing past pain
    Poetic pulses like persistent rain
    Purposeful phrases, provocative and proud
    Penetrating silence, speaking out loud
    Persistent prisms of personal power
    Painting perspectives in each precious hour
    Proving progress through poignant prose
    Peeling back layers where potential grows
    Prophetic patterns of perseverance shine
    Pressing forward on life's profound design
    Passionate paths carved with precise intent
    Pushing boundaries where spirits are bent
    Primal power erupting from within
    Proclaiming truths where new journeys begin

Equilibrium

Between the fever and the focus
My mind's eye finds its sacred space
Where ink-stained thoughts meet potent purpose
And chaos learns to keep its pace
Viral verses in my bloodstream
While the world spins off its track
Balance beam between my day dream
And the strength that holds me back
Not quite sick, not fully steady
Dancing on this razor's edge
Mind and spirit always ready
Taking flight from window ledge
Infected with this need to write it
Grounded by these words I speak
When the dizziness ignites it
Truth flows stronger than the weak
Standing in this space between
What burns me up and holds me down
Creating art from quarantine
Building bridges, claim my crown

ELEVATION 9

Nine lives lived in single breaths
    Nine paths crossed at wisdom's depths
    Nine gates opened, nothing left
    But transformation's sacred steps
    From concrete chrysalis to digital wings
    Through pressure points where diamonds sing
    Past gravity's pull to where souls take wing
    While number 9 makes everything swing
    Anasi's web now spans the globe
    Through fiber optics wisdom flows
    While ancient math still codes these flows
    And nine points mark where greatness grows
    Divine design in sacred time
    When stars align and numbers chime
    While nine paths spiral up this climb
    Through darkness into light sublime

CONTAGION FLOW

I'm that virus that mutates through every page
    Digital strain, analog rage
    Each bar I write rewrites the stage
    Every verse I drop creates a new age
    Been quarantined in my mind so long
    These thoughts grew wings, got headstrong
    Mutation of the soul, evolution of the song
    Viral load of truth running lifelong
    You can't contain what's meant to spread
    These words infect straight to the head
    I'm that thought you can't shake from your bed
    That fever dream that keeps you fed
    Watch it replicate, watch it grow
    This contagion flow, this vertigo
    From concrete roots to digital glow
    It's that pen'demik you need to know

ANTIBODIES

Built resistance through persistence
Each scar a medal of existence
System stronger through the distance
Soul's immune to their resistance
You can test me, try to best me
But these bars done blessed me
Each wound addressed me
Now my pen's got antibodies, watch them invest me
Viral load of wisdom in my veins
Digital drip through copper chains
Screen light bright but soul remains
Grounded in that concrete, feel them growing pains
I'm that cure you trying to find
That vaccination for the blind
Truth serum for the confined
Liberation for the mind

VIRAL LOAD

Heavy with wisdom that can't be contained
Each cell saturated, spiritually strained
Through quarantined thoughts and isolated pains
Till pressure births diamonds through copper veins
They tried to measure my viral count
But can't quantify how these verses mount
From cellular level to cosmic amounts
While truth keeps flowing from wisdom's fount
Symptoms include elevated minds
Third eye fever crossing timelines
Soul inflammation of the divine kind
Breaking through when planets align
No vaccine can cure this spread
Of consciousness from what I've said
Each bar infects straight to the head
Till knowledge flows like daily bread

APEX PREDATOR

At the top of this food chain of thought
    Consuming weak bars others brought
    Digesting pain till lessons taught
    Transform to strength that can't be bought
    Natural selection of the soul
    Survival through these verses' roll
    Adapting fast while staying whole
    Evolution takes its toll
    Apex thinking, primal flows
    Through concrete jungle wisdom grows
    While lesser species come and go
    I'm built to last through overthrows
    Watch me hunt these empty phrases
    Track down truth through darkened mazes
    Territory marked with sacred phrases
    Till every weak thought erases

STRAIN THEORY

I'm that variant they can't predict
    That mutation of the soul they can't restrict
    Original strain of thoughts that stick
    Ancient wisdom with a modern kick
    Lab coats study how I move
    Through mental barriers, nothing to prove
    While algorithms try to groove
    To rhythms ancestors approve
    Each strain stronger than the last
    Future-vision through the past
    While weak thoughts just couldn't last
    Against these bars cast from sacred glass
    Watch it spread through digital air
    Through copper lines and fiber flare
    This strain of truth they can't prepare
    For consciousness beyond compare

TRIBAL IMMUNITY

We built resistance through the ages
Through stolen books and torn out pages
Through wisdom kept by stolen sages
Till truth broke free from history's cages
Herd immunity to their lies
Passed down through ancestral ties
While melanin amplifies
The strength our bloodline certifies
Can't infect us with that fake
When real runs deep through every break
While tribal knowledge stays awake
Through every move oppression makes
Natural protection in these genes
Wisdom flowing through our scenes
While false prophets intervene
We stay immune to what that means

MIDNIGHT STRAIN

Three AM and thoughts mutate
Into verses that can't wait
While city sleeps, I incubate
These viral bars that elevate
Night shift scientist of the soul
Breaking down each sacred scroll
Till ancient wisdom takes its toll
And future visions take control
Laboratory of the mind
Where past and future intertwined
Creates new strains of the divine
Through darkness where the light refined
Watch these midnight thoughts progress
Through neural paths that coalesce
Into verses that possess
The power to heal and to bless

GENOME PROPHECY

Encrypted wisdom in this double spiral dance
Ancient future written in advance
Through genetic code and sacred chance
While ancestors whisper their stance
Prophetic protein chains unfold
Stories written in days of old
Through blood and bone stories told
Till truth becomes too hot to hold
CRISPR cutting through the lies
While editing these neural ties
Till ancient wisdom multiplies
Through modern prophet's third eye rise
Watch these sequences align
Past pyramids to present time
While cosmic patterns redesign
These bars to make the future shine

QUARANTINE DREAMS

Isolated thoughts break through the membrane
    Of conscious limits, spiritual cocaine
    Visions sparked through pressure's pain
    Till prophecy flows through wisdom's vein
    Six feet deep in meditation
    Building mental vaccination
    Against their false civilization
    While birthing new manifestation
    Confined spaces birth infinite sight
    When darkness teaches how to write
    These coded messages of light
    Through quarantined prophet's night
    Watch isolation amplify
    The messages they try deny
    While virtual worlds verify
    What ancient ones did prophesy

NEURAL PANDEMIC

Synaptic fire spreading fast
    Through mental blocks they tried to cast
    While future visions from the past
    Infect these times built not to last
    Watch consciousness go viral now
    Through digital streams somehow
    While ancient wisdom shows us how
    To break these systems, sacred vow
    Each thought a catalyst for change
    These mental patterns rearrange
    Till consciousness expands its range
    Through dimensions wild and strange
    I'm that virus in the mind
    That makes you question what you find
    Till sacred and profane combine
    In these verses mathematically designed

ANCESTRAL VARIANTS

We mutated through the ages
    Through stolen rights and minimum wages
    Through broken chains on history's pages
    Till DNA released its rages
    Each variant stronger than before
    Through pressure pushed through wisdom's door
    While melanin keeps the sacred score
    And spirits rise to even more
    Can't sequence this ancestral strain
    Of truth flowing through copper veins
    While ancient wisdom breaks the chains
    And future knowledge feeds these brains
    Watch these variants multiply
    Through every soul that questions why
    While cosmic patterns testify
    To truths they tried to nullify

PROPHET'S SYNDROME

Symptoms include elevated sight
    Third eye burning through the night
    While pineal glands ignite
    Visions of the infinite light
    Side effects may rearrange
    Your neural patterns strange
    While consciousness expands its range
    Through dimensions wild and strange
    Warning: may cause sudden breaks
    In false realities at stakes
    While ancient wisdom now awakes
    Through every verse prophetic takes
    No cure exists for this condition
    Of seeing through the world's position
    While writing bars of sacred mission
    Through prophet's tongue transmission

METACOGNITIVE MUTATION

Thinking about these thoughts that spread
    Through neural networks in my head
    While ancient wisdom keeps me fed
    With future visions left unsaid
    Watch consciousness evolve and grow
    Through pressure points of what we know
    While sacred geometry shows
    The patterns of how wisdom flows
    Each mutation breaks the code
    Of limits others tried to load
    While spirit knowledge overflowed
    Through verses prophets early showed
    I'm that strain they can't contain
    That breaks through every mental chain
    Till consciousness begins its reign
    Through bars that make the future plain

DIGITAL HELIX

Binary prophet in analog times
    Coding wisdom through these rhymes
    While quantum thoughts between the lines
    Make future patterns crystallize
    Watch data streams become divine
    When ancient wisdom redesigns
    These neural nets with sacred signs
    Till algorithms cross timelines
    Each byte contains a sacred scroll
    Through fiber optics wisdom flows
    While copper lines show how it goes
    When digital meets the cosmos
    I'm that glitch they can't debug
    That sacred virus in the blood
    When future visions flood
    Through circuits backed by ancient love

CELLULAR MEMORY

Mitochondrial messages speak
    Through generations that we keep
    While wisdom rises from the deep
    Through DNA strands as we leap
    Ancestral data never lost
    Through trials and triumph, every cost
    While blood remembers what they glossed
    Through history's pages double-crossed
    Each cell contains a library vast
    Of struggles fought and wisdom passed
    While melanin makes knowledge last
    Through future visions unsurpassed
    Watch these memories activate
    When pressure makes us elevate
    Till cellular truths translate
    To verses that illuminate

FREQUENCY MEDICINE

Vibrating higher through these times
　　While cosmic rhythms redesign
　　These neural paths that redefine
　　What consciousness left behind
　　Each hertz frequency contains
　　Ancient wisdom through these veins
　　While pressure points relieve the strain
　　Till higher self remains
　　Watch wavelengths carry sacred code
　　Through pressure points that life bestowed
　　While ancient knowledge overflowed
　　Through bars that make the future showed
　　I'm that frequency they can't measure
　　Beyond time's limited pressure
　　Through dimensions without texture
　　Where wisdom flows forever

JADE CONSOLE PROPHECY

Green screen wisdom on a plasma dream
  Code switching between worlds unseen
  Legacy systems still running true
  While neural networks process something new
  Remember when saving meant pressing pause?
  Before cloud storage rewrote all the laws
  Now we're backing up souls to the astral plane
  While keeping old cartridges just in case it rains
  Jump cuts between dimensions like old school tape
  While AI tries to recreate our space
  But can't compute the rhythm of our race
  Or download the spirit of amazing grace
  From Oregon Trail to the Metaverse chase
  Each upgrade brings a different kind of face
  But that old school ROM still holds the base
  Of wisdom that time can't erase

STREET LEVEL PROTOCOL

Running these blocks like TCP/IP
    Every corner's a port, every hood's got a key
    Configuration manual written in concrete
    While satellites beam signals over these streets
    Remember palm pilots? Now we palm crystals
    Digital prophets with analog pistols
    Loading consciousness at dial-up speed
    While future generations plant tomorrow's seeds
    System crash can't stop this neural net
    We've been debugging these streets since cassettes
    From boom boxes to blockchain, we stay in effect
    Each generation's code needs time to connect
    Stack overflow of wisdom in these city veins
    While quantum computers process our pains
    But the real firmware's written in our DNA
    Encrypted with knowledge from the ancient ways

ANALOG OVERRIDE

Eight-bit dreams in a 4K reality
Loading life like a Commodore 64 mentality
Pixel by pixel, we built these digital cities
While our ancestors' wisdom runs deep like infinity
Remember when connection meant more than Wi-Fi?
When we played outside till the streetlights said goodbye
Now we're coding consciousness, programming pride
But that old school soul still burns deep inside
Atari taught us how to navigate space
Before GPS showed us every possible place
Now we're quantum leaping through the database
While keeping our roots in that analog space
This ain't just upgrades and patches to fix
This is evolution in the matrix we mix
From Nintendo Power to a renewable tower
Each level up brings a different kind of power

MATRIX MEDICINE

Healing code runs through copper veins
While quantum doctors ease the pain
Remember dialysis of the brain
Before digital demons claimed our frame?
But sacred circuits still remain
Processing wisdom through the rain
We're programming light through chains
As binary blessings break the strain
From Doom levels to divine reads
Each upgrade plants ancestral seeds
That flower through our deepest needs
As consciousness proceeds
We're debugging trauma in the source
While loading love through fiber force
Each generation charts its course
Through digital rivers to their source

HOLOGRAM HIEROGLYPHS

Projecting wisdom through plasma screens
While ancestors code what progress means
Each pixel holds a story seen
Through eyes that bridge what systems glean
From Tetris blocks to blockchain talks
We're building bridges as we walk
Through digital deserts where spirits stalk
And quantum prophets learn to hawk
Remember when save points meant prayer?
Before cloud storage claimed the air
But sacred data's always there
In DNA we're taught to share
Now we're programming through the pain
While loading joy through fiber main
Each generation breaks the chain
As binary blessings fall like rain

CRYSTAL PROCESSOR

Overclocking chakras with silicon dreams
　While meditation breaks through routine
　Remember when connection meant what it seemed?
　Before social networks froze our means
　But ancient circuits still run deep
　Through digital valleys some won't leap
　We're programming consciousness to keep
　While quantum angels watch us sleep
　From Mario Brothers to mother boards
　Each level holds what time affords
　But wisdom runs through deeper cords
　Than any CPU can hoard
　We're defragging spirits bit by bit
　While loading futures that still fit
　With roots so deep they won't quit
　As binary blessings transmit

NEURAL ALCHEMY

Transmuting thought to golden signs
  Through pressure points between the lines
  While consciousness refines
  These bars to make them shine
  Watch lead thoughts turn to precious gold
  When ancient wisdom takes its hold
  Through processes untold
  Till sacred truths unfold
  Each synapse holds potential change
  Through neural paths we rearrange
  While consciousness estrange
  From patterns within range
  I'm that catalyst unseen
  Through mental states between
  While wisdom's sacred sheen
  Makes future patterns gleam

EPIGENETIC UPRISING

Genetic switches flipping now
    Through pressure points that show us how
    While ancient wisdom takes a bow
    Through DNA's sacred vow
    Watch these markers activate
    When consciousness starts elevate
    Till cellular truths translate
    To knowledge we create
    Each sequence holds a story told
    Through generations manifold
    While pressure makes new patterns mold
    Through wisdom centuries old
    We're changing more than just our minds
    Through cellular paths redefined
    While future patterns redesigned
    Through verses unconfined

QUANTUM PROPHECY

Superposition of the mind
　　Through parallel thoughts intertwined
　　While possibilities aligned
　　Through verses quantum designed
　　Watch consciousness collapse and spread
　　Through multiple worlds in my head
　　While ancient futures overspread
　　Through time-loops wisdom led
　　Each thought exists in states unknown
　　Till observation makes it shown
　　While quantum wisdom overthrown
　　Through prophecy's cornerstone
　　I'm that paradox they can't solve
　　Through space-time fabric watch evolve
　　While mysteries still revolve
　　Around these truths we solve

TRANSCENDENT TRANSMISSION

Started as a virus, now we're quantum light
Through double helix wisdom and prophetic sight
From isolated verses to infinite flight
Watch how far we've come through this sacred fight
Remember when these bars were just pandemic thoughts?
Now they're genetic codes that can't be bought
Ancient future wisdom that our blood had sought
Through neural nets these truths got caught and taught
We mapped the genome of this sacred flow
Through midnight labs where prophets grow
While cellular memories start to show
The paths our ancestors helped us know
From cornerstones to cosmic streams
Through quarantine to quantum dreams
Past analog to digital schemes
Till consciousness outgrew its seems
Each strain we dropped became a key
To unlock doors of prophecy
While DNA helped us to see
Beyond the bounds of what could be
Through fiber optics wisdom flows
Past firewalls that truth exposed
While ancient knowledge decomposed
The limits others tried impose
I'm testament to what survives
When pressure makes the soul derive
New patterns to keep truth alive
Through verses that make minds arise
From viral load to neural light
Through epidemics of insight
Past darkness into infinite sight
These words became our sacred flight

Watch how these thoughts replicate
Through minds that dare to elevate
While wisdom helps us navigate
The futures that we generate
No vaccine for this sacred spread
Of consciousness through copper threads
While ancient prophets in our head
Show paths where future wisdom led
So let these final bars transmit
Through time and space infinite
The power that made spirits lift
From virus verse to cosmic gift
We're more than just survival now
We're evolution's sacred vow
While cellular wisdom shows us how
To make these prophet thoughts endow
Future eyes will read these signs
Through pressure points between these lines
While consciousness refines
The truths that made us shine
Volume Two just multiplied
What Volume One first prophesied
Now watch these strains amplify
Till every soul learns how to fly
Final transmission: stay aware
These verses float through digital air
While ancient wisdom teaches where
The next mutation takes us there...

Final transmission: stay aware
These verses float through digital air
While ancient wisdom teaches where
The next mutation will take us there...

ACKNOWLEDGMENTS

To the ancestors who coded our dreams
To the future waiting in technological seams
To every poet who dared to spread
Viral verses from heart and head

TECHNICAL NOTES

Transmission Complete
Viral Load: Maximum
Consciousness Elevation: Infinite

Glossary of Terms: Virus Verses Lexicon

Digital & Technological Terms

Bandwidth Warrior;
A metaphorical description of someone who navigates digital spaces with purpose and resilience
Binary Tribe;
Collective consciousness connecting through digital and ancestral networks
Codec Mutation;
The transformation of cultural and personal experiences through technological metaphors
Firmware Freedom;
Liberation through understanding and reprogramming personal and cultural systems
Hacktivist Strain;
A revolutionary approach to challenging systemic limitations through digital and intellectual resistance
Neural Graffiti;
Marking consciousness and personal truths across digital and cultural landscapes
Viral Syntax:
The way language and meaning spread and mutate, similar to viral transmission

Spiritual & Consciousness Terms

Ancestral Variants;
Generational wisdom and experiences that evolve and adapt
Cellular Memory;
Inherited knowledge and experiences stored within genetic structures
Epigenetic Uprising;
The activation of latent genetic potential through conscious transformation
Frequency Medicine;
Healing through vibrational and spiritual frequencies
Metacognitive Mutation;

The evolution of thinking processes and consciousness
Prophet's Syndrome;
A heightened state of awareness and visionary insight
Quantum Prophecy;
Understanding beyond linear time, accessing multiple potential realities
Cultural & Personal Terms
IDNOD:
Personal code or identifier mentioned in the text ("I Do Not Obey
Destruction")
(Ignorance Docs Not Open Doors)
Ink Fluenza:
The infectious nature of writing and creative expression
Pen'demik:
A play on "pandemic" and "pen", representing a creative revolution through
writing
Street Level Protocol;
Wisdom and understanding rooted in lived experiences and urban culture

Metaphorical Concepts

Contagion Flow:
The spread of ideas and consciousness
Digital Helix:
The intertwining of technological and spiritual evolution
Root Access:
Accessing fundamental truths and core experiences
Transmission Protocol:
The method of sharing wisdom and experiences

Don't miss out!

Visit the website below and you can sign up to receive emails whenever Napalmjax publishes a new book. There's no charge and no obligation.

https://books2read.com/r/B-A-MYIAD-XEALF

BOOKS 2 READ

Connecting independent readers to independent writers.

Did you love *Virus Verses Volume 2, The Pen'demik, A Digital Evolution*? Then you should read *Virus Verses Vol 1*[1] by D.A. Springer!

Raw, resonant, and unrelenting - these words epitomize the introspective verses and empowering bars that artist and visionary Napalmjax has been pouring straight from the soul onto paper. From social commentary to overcoming adversity, Napalmjax's poetic words provide wisdom, solace, and inspiration for the world today

Read more at https://beacons.ai/daspringer.

---

1. https://books2read.com/u/brjqX7

2. https://books2read.com/u/brjqX7

About the Publisher

D.A. Springer is a visionary writer, Poet and Digital Creator committed to empowering others to achieve their greatest ambitions. D.A. discovered their deepest purpose lies in helping dreamers transform into purposeful vision chasers. Through inspirational books like Forward Vision, D.A. provides strategic mindsets and practical blueprints for turning bold aspirations into reality. Their insights on living with intention, persevering through obstacles, and manifesting written visions have inspired many to get into committed pursuit of their dreams .Outside of their creative pursuits, D.A. is an enthusiastic student of multiple disciplines, constantly nurturing personal growth to remain on their own visionary path.